Would You Like a Joke?

Book 5

A 'Dad Joke' collection

Dave Anderson

Copyright – Disclaimer

Introduction

With a twinkle in his eye, and a smirk on his face, everyone knew a joke was on the way. This is how my father introduced me to the world of humor. His mother introduced her family to humor, and it was shared by Glen and his five sisters.

His two younger sisters were well practiced in the craft. When the girls got going, they could keep the family laughing for hours. Precious family memories.

The goal of this book, is to give the readers some jokes that they can enjoy, and share with others. Humor and laughter are good medicine.

ENJOY!

Acknowledgments

Most parents agree: parents should embarrass their children. My children say that I took the embarrass idea to the extreme. Admittedly, that is probably true. All the while, I was perfecting my ability to tell jokes. It helped me realize that seeing people laugh is what truly gives me happiness.

As I deliver pizza, my Manager gives me the freedom to offer my customers a joke at the door. This has allowed me to practice and refine my jokes, while providing a more personal service than normal and expected.

Dedication

Before my first Semester in College, I participated in a Physical Education course entitled, "Wilderness Challenge." This was three weeks of backpacking and canoeing in the Boundary Waters Canoe Area of N E Minnesota.

There were ten guys in our group. There was an Upper-Class student who was familiar with the BWCA. He was an advisor and would take over in case of emergency. In a wilderness area it is important to take all precautions.

The first half of our trip was the backpacking phase. When everything that is needed is being carried in your backpacks, there is no room for anything that is not absolutely necessary. As a result, the provisions were sparse. With all of the physical activity involved, virtually everything that was eaten was burned up on a daily basis. Everything was shared with the group of ten guys. The only exception to this was the one-per-day Salted Nut Roll that each guy was carrying in his pack.

When we changed from backpacking to canoeing, it was well known that we would get a resupply of provisions. As some of the guys *may* have eaten more than one Salted Nut Roll in a day, the Salted Nut Roll became an item of barter. "If you give me one Salted Nut Roll today, you can have two of my Salted Nut Rolls on resupply," was the typical barter conversation.

The advisors had given the final assignment. Our group decided to push the final leg. This would give us some rest at base camp before the final run. The final run was slated to be 10 miles, cross country style.

On one of the last days on our push, we arrived at beautiful Rose Lake in late afternoon.   To get to Rose Lake we went DOWN Staircase Portage. We saw a beautiful rainbow. Some guys did some fishing. We slept in the cabin there. We even had real beds. A very pleasant evening.

In the morning we had to go UP Staircase Portage. We had all of our gear and canoes. At a landing on the Staircase, I was totally spent.

My buddy Dave then did one of the nicest things anyone has ever done for me. He reached in his pack and found one of his Salted Nut Rolls. He gave me HIS precious Salted Nut Roll. He said I needed it. He was right about that. I was totally exhausted. Mentally. Physically. Emotionally. EXHAUSTED!

Thank you, Dave Steeves, for being a part of my life since August, 1979.

1

When Mom returned to the room, how do we know the preschooler was in trouble?

The writing was on the wall!

2

What happened when the orchard truck was forced off the road?

The apple cart was upset.

3

Why did the inventory-taker become a negotiator?

They wanted to hear the counter offer.

4

Why did the bowler think they had won all of the games?

They heard they were going to the Super Bowl.

5

What did the dishes say to the dishwasher?

We are soaked!

6

What did the Panama Canal lock say to the ship?

I'm going to let you down easy.

7

What did the pearl say to the oyster?

Am I irritating you?

8

When they are outside, what do you call a vape shop customer?

A vaper in the wind.

9

On the drying rack, what did one dish say to the other dish?

Don't be a drip.

10

How did the plan die?

It was put to the committee.

Wait for it. . .

It was executed.

11

Why did the Retailer place a carpenter's square near the Front Counter?

They wanted to corner their market.

12

In the Old West town, why were the salon and the saloon next to each other?

Either way, everybody looks better when they are done.

13

How was the 'on fire' athlete like a record player?

They are in the groove.

14

Why did the Funeral Home reserve a spot in the cemetery?

They were plotting the death of their customers.

15

How did the roofer indicate that they were in Business?

They hung out their shingle.

16

Why was the archery range easily approved?

Everything was right on target.

17

Why was the person looking for their watch?

They had lost track of time.

18

Before going out into the world, why did the young lady put on high heels?

She didn't want to be caught flat-footed.

19

Why was the person wearing so many watches?

They wanted to have more time on their hands.

20

Why did the Archbishop go on the radio?

They wanted a Mass audience.

21

Why did the landscape worker get in trouble?

They were always beating around the bush.

22

What did the radio announcer say to their producer?

You're pushing my buttons.

23

Why was the milk jug leaking?

It couldn't contain itself.

24

What happened to the Scotsman's dog?

He kilt it.

25

If I move that object,

Will you object?

26

What happened to the ceramic bowl?

It got fired up.

27

Why did the sewing machine operator choose a heavy-duty needle?

To be sure they could get through thick or thin.

28

What did the person say when they put the frozen pizza in the oven?

Rack 'em up.

29

Why did the person go to the lube shop?

They wanted some elbow grease.

30

Why did the Retriever dog NOT go 1/2 mile for the bird?

That was just too far-fetched.

To be continued. . .

Power of Humor

While delivering the pizza, an amazing thing happens with the jokes.

My customer may say that I look familiar. If it is not time for the joke, I will normally reply, "We will find out in a minute." When the transaction is complete, I will ask my now-famous question: "Would you like an original joke today?"

"**NOW** I remember you," is the typical response.

On other occasions, when I ask my question, the customer may reply, "Yes, you told me a joke last time, and it was a good one."

Other customers recognize me and ask ME for a joke.

Still other customers may say something like, "Every time you deliver to me you have a joke, and it's always different."

The response that I will always remember, was the delivery I made to a customer I had never seen before. At the end of the delivery, he looked at me and said, "That was the BEST delivery I have ever had!"

People remember that you offered them a joke, and that it was not offensive in any way. THAT is the power of humor.

Thank you!

We have many choices in our World these days. Thank you for choosing this book. It is hoped that you enjoyed it, and my unique brand of humor.

To contact Dave, email
summitdave56@yahoo.com

To find more books in this series, for tips for Sales Professionals and to see other projects, visit
www.summitdave.com

Normally it would say to expect a new book in a few months. To catch up, however, it will only be a few weeks.

Biography

Dave Anderson was raised on a farm near Summit, South Dakota. He was introduced to jokes and humor by his father, Glen. When they saw that particular smirk and grin, everyone knew Glen was telling a joke. This was passed on to Dave and his siblings.

After High School, Dave joined the U S Air Force, being stationed in Tacoma, Washington. After the four-year enlistment, Dave attended College and attained a B A.

Dave landed in Milwaukee, Wisconsin, raising a daughter and son. Delivering pizza, he developed the service of offering a joke to his customers. Creating his own jokes, his customers suggested that he write a book. This continues the 'Dad Joke' series.